GRIEF'S MELODY

KARTHIK KOPPI

To the ones I love and trust,
Your faith in me has been my strength through every storm.

And to Lord Krishna,
For guiding me through the battle within and beyond.

Contents

Contents

Contents

Foreword

Life is not a straight path, it twists and turns through light and shadow, joy and sorrow, love and pain. Grief's Melody is a reflection of this journey, a collection of poems that seeks to give voice to the unspoken feelings that shape us. Grief, love, hope, pain, loss, and redemption, each poem is a note in the symphony of existence, resonating with the quiet moments we often carry alone.

This book is not merely a series of poems; it is a mirror held up to the human soul. It explores the fragile beauty of vulnerability, the quiet strength found in despair, and the fleeting grace of happiness. Pain leaves its mark on every heart, carving deep wounds that only time and understanding can heal. Each verse is a heartbeat, echoing the timeless struggle between holding on and letting go.

I hope that as you turn these pages, you find fragments of your own story in these words. May these poems remind you that even in the depths of grief and pain, there is music, and in that music, a quiet promise of healing.

Let this melody accompany you through the highs and lows of life. And may you find, in these words, the courage to face both the darkness and the dawn.

Let the melody begin.

-Karthik koppi.

Preface

Life is a symphony of emotions. joy, sorrow, love, and loss, all woven together into a melody that defines who we are. Grief's Melody is born from the quiet moments of reflection, from the unspoken words that linger in the heart long after the world has moved on. This collection of poems is not merely an exploration of grief but a journey through the spectrum of human experience on pain, healing, longing, and acceptance.

Grief is not always loud; sometimes, it whispers through the silence of the night, through the absence of a familiar presence, or the weight of memories that refuse to fade. In these poems, I have tried to capture those subtle echoes, the heaviness of heartache and the quiet strength that emerges from it. Each verse reflects the rawness of loss, the tenderness of love, and the quiet resilience that grief often leaves behind.

Grief's Melody is not just about mourning; it's about understanding. It's about finding beauty in brokenness, solace in solitude, and strength in vulnerability. Through these words, I hope to reach those who have felt the ache of loss, the sting of disappointment, and the emptiness that follows. But more than that, I hope this book serves as a reminder that healing is not linear and that grief, in its own haunting way, can teach us how to love more deeply and live more fully.

This is my heart laid bare, each poem a fragment of my soul, a reflection of moments that shaped me. I offer this to you, the reader, not as a solution to grief, but as a companion through it. May you find pieces of yourself in these lines and may they remind you that even in sorrow, there is a quiet melody waiting to be heard.

-Karthik koppi.

Acknowledgements

Writing Grief's Melody has been a deeply personal and emotional journey that would not have been possible without the support and inspiration of several people who have touched my life in profound ways.

First and foremost, I want to express my deepest gratitude to my family for their unwavering love and understanding. Your strength gave me the courage to explore the depths of my emotions and put them into words. Thank you for standing by me even when I struggled to find the right words.

To my friends, your presence, patience, and quiet encouragement have provided comfort through the highs and lows. Thank you for listening, for understanding the silence between the words, and for reminding me that even in grief, there is space for laughter and hope.

A special thanks to those who have shared their stories of loss and healing with me. Your vulnerability and honesty helped me see grief not as an end but as a bridge toward deeper understanding and growth. Your experiences are woven into the heart of this book.

To the unseen moments of inspiration, the quiet nights, the forgotten conversations, and the memories that resurfaced when I least expected them, thank you for shaping these poems into what they are.

Finally, to you, the reader, thank you for picking up this book and allowing these words to become a part of your journey. I hope you find solace, understanding, and perhaps even a little healing within these pages.

With heartfelt gratitude,

-Karthik koppi.

Prologue

Grief is not loud. It does not arrive with a warning or leave when asked. It slips in quietly through the empty spaces left behind by someone's absence, through the quiet ache that settles in your chest when you wake up to a world that feels incomplete. It lingers in the shadows of forgotten conversations, in the places where laughter once lived, and in the silence that follows goodbye.

There was a time when I thought grief was something you could outrun that time would soften its edges and blur the sharpness of loss. But I've learned that grief is not meant to be conquered; it's meant to be carried. It becomes a part of you, reshaping you in ways you don't always understand. It teaches you to hold on, to let go, and sometimes to do both at the same time.

This book is not about finding answers. It's about the questions we ask when grief settles in, the quiet "why" that echoes in the night, the silent prayers whispered into the void, and the longing for things we cannot change. It's about the slow, painful process of learning to breathe again when the weight of absence makes it hard to draw air.

Grief's Melody is the echo of a heart that loved deeply and lost painfully. Each poem in these pages is a reflection of that love, a melody born from sorrow but carried forward by hope.

This is my attempt to make sense of the weight we all carry. And maybe, just maybe, you'll find a piece of your own story within these lines.

1. Painted in Joy

Colors dance upon laughing skin,
Washing away where hate has been.
Enemies smile, strangers embrace,
Lost in the magic of color and grace.

Red for love, fierce and deep,
Green for hope that dares to leap.
Yellow for warmth, bright as the sun,
Blue for calm when the day is done.
Hands stained with pink and gold,
Stories of friendship, new and old.
Laughter floats upon the breeze,
Hearts unchained, spirits at ease.

Like Holi's hues, life's never plain,
Sunshine and storms, joy and pain.
Colors fade, but memories stay,
Teaching us light will find its way.
Smear the past with shades anew,
Let go of gray, embrace the blue.
Forgive, forget &rise above,
Let every color remind you of love.

2. Masterpiece

I am a storm with painted skies,
A fire that burns but never dies.
A paradox of dark and light,
A restless soul that craves the night.
My heart's a map of scars and gold,
A story wild, untamed, untold.
A whisper soft, a thunder loud,
A fleeting dream, a gathering cloud.

I rise, I fall, I break, I mend,
A curse, a blessing, both transcend.
A hurricane with fragile grace,
A war, a waltz, a sweet embrace.
I love too deep, I heal, I harm,
A shattered soul with boundless charm.
A chaos wrapped in silk and lace,
A masterpiece of flaws I chase.

So call me wreckage, call me art,
A contradiction torn apart.
For in my ruin, I have found,
A beauty fierce, yet unbound.

3. Unseen, Unheard, Unheld

I chased the stars, I fought the rain,
Wore every scar, embraced the pain.
My hands reached out, but touched the night,
While you stood still, beneath the light.

I spoke in silence, screamed in peace,
Gave you my calm, my wild release.
Yet every gift fell through the cracks,
A fading echo, lost in black.

I climbed the walls of your guarded heart,
Sought warmth within, found only dark.
My love, a song you wouldn't hear,
My presence, just a passing year.

No matter how I stood or knelt,
No matter all the love I felt,
Efforts bloom where hearts align,
But yours was never meant for mine.

So now I stand where silence reigns,
A quiet grave of hopes and pain.
For love is not a war to win,
When you are not the one within.

4. The Heart That Stays

I am not difficult to love,
I just want love to feel like home,
a place where hearts are held with care,
where I am seen, not left alone.

I do not ask for silver moons,
nor grand displays that fade with time,
just hands that reach when mine feel cold,
and love that stays steady, sublime.

I give my love in ways so pure,
with open arms, with words that heal,
with whispers soft, with quiet strength,
with all the depths my soul can feel.

I don't demand a perfect tale,
just honesty, just warmth, just trust.
A love that mirrors what I give,
not fleeting sparks, but embers' dust.

So if my love feels like too much,
perhaps it's not for you to hold.
But know that when it finds its home,
it turns the simple into gold.

5. A Heart Set on Fire

What is that love, if it brings no pain?
A hollow breeze, a passing rain.
If the heart beats calm, untouched, unfazed,
Can it be love or just a passing haze?

Love should burn, like fire at night,
A restless storm, a hopeless fight.
It carves its mark, deep in the soul,
Leaving behind scars that never grow whole.

What is that love, if tears don't fall?
If silence doesn't echo through each call?
If the chest doesn't tighten with aching breath,
Can it be love or just a shadow of death?

Love should be madness, raw and wild,
A curse, a blessing, both cruel and mild.
It should tear you apart, yet make you whole,
An endless war between heart and soul.

So tell me, what is that love, if it brings no pain?
A passing cloud, a forgotten name.
For true love bleeds, and true love burns.
And from that fire, the heart returns.

6. Forged in the Fire

The sky may darken, winds may cry,
The road may break, yet still you try.
The weight you bear, the scars you gain,
All whisper low, endure the pain.

The fire that burns within your chest,
Is forging strength, a heart possessed.
Through shattered dreams and nights so long,
You rise again, a warrior's song.
For every tear the heavens take,
Returns as gold the dawn will wake.
The wounds you fear, the past you blame,
Are carving out a brighter name.

So let the storm, let sorrow reign,
But know this truth, it's not in vain.
Through every trial, through loss and strain,
There lies a purpose in the pain.

7. Between Fire and Chains

I walk a path where dreams reside,
Yet shadows whisper by my side.
A bridge between the stars and ground,
Where silent echoes of fate resound.
Hope is a flame that flickers bright,
A promise carved in golden light.
It paints the skies with hues so bold,
Yet slips through fingers, hard to hold.
Reality stands with anchored feet,
A bitter truth, a steady beat.
It speaks in terms of stone and steel,
Of what is lost and what is real.
Between the two, I drift, I sway,
A restless soul in night and day.
One hand on fire, one bound in chains,
A heart that beats in love and pain.
Do llet go or dare to dream?
To chase the sun or wade the stream?
Or find my place where both align,
Where hope and truth no longer bind?

8. No Longer the Same

The one you left wore fragile skin,
A quiet storm, a war within.
His voice was soft, steps unsure,
A heart that bled but still endured.

You turned away, you closed the door,
And He stood shattered on the floor.
But from the cracks, the light broke through,
And He became someone you never knew.

The tears you saw are rivers dried,
Replaced by fire I now confide.
The shadows fled, I claimed my ground,
In silence, strength is often found.

Now look again, if you dare,
The one you knew is no longer there.
The one you left was someone else,
Now come back and see, I am someone else.

9. Echoes in the Rain

How could you give up so easily,
When the storms had just begun to wane?
Did the echoes of our shared laughter,
Fade too soon, swallowed by the rain?
How did you not find a reason to stay,
When our world still carried your name?
Were the roots we planted too shallow,
Or was I alone in tending the flame?

I am tired, fighting this battle alone,
Building walls against silence and despair.
Each breath feels heavy, each step unsure,
In a world where you no longer care.

Was it so easy to turn and leave,
To let go of promises, fragile yet true?
While I, still bound by the weight of hope,
Keep searching for remnants of you.

But perhaps your absence will teach me this,
That strength isn't found in holding tight,
But in knowing when to let go of hands,
That chose the dark instead of the light.

10. Shades of Gray

What is the price of loving so deep?
A heart that wakes but never sleeps.
A soul that gives, that hopes, that yearns,
Yet in return, just ashes burn.

It costs you trust, it costs you grace,
It leaves a shadow, an empty space.
The warmth you gave, now cold and still,
A heart once full, now bound by will.

To love too much is to be burned,
To feel the ache, to watch and yearn.
And when it's gone, the cost is clear,
A silence born from lingering fear.

For when you love and lose so wide,
You swear to never let love slide.
The price is high, but so it seems,
Never loving again becomes your dream.

The heart once free is now a cage,
Locked in the past, lost in a rage.
The price of love is hard to pay,
A lifetime spent in shades of gray.

11. When the Stars Mock

How many more sleepless nights must I bear,
With your shadow lingering everywhere?
The clock ticks loud in the empty room,
Echoing thoughts that deepen the gloom.

I count the stars, but they mock my pain,
Each one a memory, sharp and plain.
How many tears must silently fall,
Before the silence consumes it all?

The bed feels cold, the air too still,
Your absence bites, yet haunts me still.
How long will this ache be my only friend,
Before I find the peace that doesn't pretend?

I wonder, as the darkness grows steep,
How many nights before I permanently sleep?
But even in despair, a voice holds tight,
"Endure, for dawn follows every night."

12. Loving You, Losing Me

I loved you more than I loved myself,
More than the stars love the endless sky.
I gave you pieces I never gave another,
And called it love, though it bled me dry.

I placed you first in every breath,
A name that lived inside my chest.
Your joy was mine, your pain was too,
Ilost myself just holding you.

Iloved you more than the dreams I had,
More than the fears that held me back.
I built a world where you were the queen,
And left no space for anything.

But love that sways too close to fire,
Will turn to ash, then to desire.
Now here I stand, just smoke and bone,
Loving you, but all alone.

13. Melody of the Heart

Love is a song without a sound,
A rhythm that moves where peace is found.
It whispers soft through the quiet air,
A melody woven beyond compare.

No need for words, no cries, no calls,
It dances in shadows, through silent halls.
A heartbeat speaks where the echoes cease,
A hymn of trust, a vow of peace.

In the still of night, it softly sways,
In the hush of dawn, it lights new ways.
Unheard, unseen, yet pulsing deep,
A promise it makes, a bond to keep.

Let silence sing, let stillness show,
The language of love we already know.
For the loudest truth, the purest art,
Is the silent song that lives in the heart.

14. Hope and Its Sting

Hope is a dangerous, fleeting flame,
A whispered promise without a name.
It lifts you high, then lets you fall,
Yet still, you crave its siren call.

It builds a bridge where none should stand,
And draws a map in shifting sand.
It teases dreams, it feeds the fire,
But leaves you lost in its desire.

Oh, hope, you're cruel, you're bittersweet,
A battle won, a sure defeat.
You fill my heart, yet tear it too,
A fragile thread I can't undo.

And still, I have it, this burning ache,
This spark that sorrow cannot break.
For even knowing all its sting,
I cling to hope, it's everything.

15. The Path Back to You

Through winding roads and skies of gray,
What's meant for you won't drift away.
No need to rush, no need to chase,
It finds your heart, it knows its place.

The stars may hide, the moon may stray,
But what is yours will find its way.
Like rivers run to meet the sea,
Your destiny flows endlessly.

A love once lost, a dream once gone,
May circle back with the breaking dawn.
The things you seek, the things you yearn,
Will find their course, will one day return.

A love that's true, a dream so bright,
Will come to you in perfect light.
So hold your faith, let time unfold,
What's meant for you is yours to hold.

In every tear, in every prayer,
The universe is always fair.
With steady heart, with soul aligned,
What's truly yours will always find.

16. To Love, To Lose, To Rise

It takes some guts to fall, you know,
To let your guarded feelings show.
For love's a leap, a thrilling dive,
But hard to keep and keep alive.

The fall is sweet, the landing rough,
Not all who love will love enough.
It's easy dreams, but hard to stay,
When storms of life get in the way.

You give your heart, you hope, you pray,
But not all hearts will feel your way.
The love you give may not come back,
And leave you wandering off the track.

But still, we dare, we light the flame,
And risk the hurt, the loss, the shame.
For love, though fragile, holds the key,
To what we're truly meant to be.

To fall is bold, to stand is tough,
To make it last takes more than love.
It takes a will that won't let go,
Through highs and lows, through fast and slow.

So here's to those who rise above,

Who knows it takes true guts to love.
For hearts may break, but still they mend,
To make it last until the end.

• 17 •

17. A Stranger in the Mirror

I begged myself to be heartless,
To bury the dreams that wouldn't rest.
To cast aside the tender flame,
And wear a mask, not feel the same.

I whispered lies to soothe the ache,
Built walls no storm could ever break.
With every tear, I forged the steel,
A hollow heart I couldn't heal.

I walked through shadows, cold and grey,
Turned from the light of yesterday.
Each step, a wound, a plea, a cry,
To leave behind what said goodbye.

But in the mirror, who I see,
Is not the soul I wished to be.
A stranger's gaze, so fierce, so stark,
Lost in the void, bereft of spark.

I begged myself to numb the pain,
Yet traded gold for bitter chain.
And now I yearn for what I knew,
A heart that bled, but still was true.

Oh, to return, unmask, release,
To find the love, the light, the peace.

For in the struggle to be free,
I lost the one who was truly me.

• 19 •

18. Hearts Without Names

In a world of plans, so neat and tight,
It's the random souls who bring delight.
Strangers met by chance, not fate's decree,
Yet they carve a place in memory.

A shared smile on a crowded street,
The warmth of a laugh when strangers meet.
No backstory known, no past to bind,
Just moments shared, pure and kind.

A fleeting chat on a long train ride,
A helping hand when paths collide.
No names exchanged, no ties that tether,
Yet hearts connect in fleeting weather.

They teach us joy in life's small bends,
How strangers too can feel like friends.
No expectations, no roles to play,
Just human touch to light the way.

So here's to those we meet by chance,
In life's unscripted, fleeting dance.
For in their presence, we're truly free.
Random people are the best, you'll see.

19. Chasing What Hurts

I turn away from open hands,
From hearts that wait, from love that stands.
I chase the ones who never stay,
Adoring those who walk away.

I see the ones who love me true,
Yet leave their kindness out of view.
Their tender words, I let them fall,
While giving mine to none at all.

I love the pain, the endless fight,
The broken hearts, the sleepless nights.
I ache for those who care the least,
And starve the love that could have ceased.
Why am I blind to what is near?
Why trade my joy for hurt and fear?
Perhaps one day, I'll break this chain,
And love the ones who ease the pain.

20. Dancing in the Rain

Beneath the clouds, the heavens sing,
A gentle kiss from every spring.
The rain begins its sweet ballet,
And washes all my fears awa
Each drop, a whisper soft and true,
It feels like love poured down from you.
The world dissolves, just us remain,
Lost together in the dancing rain.
The rhythm falls, a sacred beat,
A symphony beneath our feet.
I twirl and spin in pure delight,
As raindrops glisten in the light.
Your love, it wraps me, warm and near,
A soothing song I long to hear.
In dancing rain, I feel complete,
With every drop, my heart's at peace.

Oh, rain, you've shown what words can't say,
That love can bloom on cloudy days.
In your embrace, I'll always stay,
Forever loved in your ballet.

21. Love and Lies

I gave my heart to hands untrue,
Thought they'd hold me the way I do.
But every touch was cold, unsure,
And left me aching, wanting more.

I fell for words, sweet lies you spun,
But every promise came undone.
Your smile was bright, but only skin,
No depth, no warmth, no fire within.

I tried to fit where I don't belong,
A love that felt so right, yet wrong.
In every glance, I hoped to find,
A trace of love, a spark, a sign.

But love with you was never safe,
A dangerous dance, a twisted faith.
And though I fought to make it stay,
I knew that love should not betray.

So now I walk, a little scared,
But wiser for the battles hard.
For love will come, not built on lies,
But steady, true, with open eyes.

22. A Dance with the Stars

Beneath the sky where stardust gleams,
She walks, a vision of whispered dreams.
Her hair flows like a midnight tide,
Soft waves where moonlit secrets hide.

Her eyes, twin lanterns of the night,
Hold galaxies, a mystic light.
Each glance she casts is a painter's hue,
A canvas alive with golden dew.

Her smile, a melody, tender and pure,
A cure for hearts that once were unsure.
Its warmth ignites a soulful spark,
A lighthouse beam in the ocean's dark.

Her voice, a breeze on a summer's day,
A soothing tune that sweeps dismay.
Each word she speaks is a poet's rhyme,
A song that halts the march of time.

Her grace defies the bounds of air,
A dance that floats with none to compare.
Each step she takes, the earth feels blessed,
As nature bows in her soft caress.

Oh, heaven must envy her radiant glow,

A flower in bloom where love will grow.
For in her presence, the world stands still,
Her beauty, a wonder no words could fulfil.

23. To the Earth, To the Sky

I belong to the skies, where the winds are free,
To the rivers that sing, and the unbound sea.
I belong to the butterflies, fragile and light,
To the dawn's soft whisper, the embrace of night.

I belong to the forests, where shadows dance,
To the wild, green glades in a secret trance.
I belong to the flowers, to the roots, to the rain,
To the whispers of nature, in joy and in pain.

I belong to the mountains, to the earth's steady breath,
To the life and the quiet that follow death.
I belong to the echoes that wander the lea,
A wanderer, a dreamer, eternally free.

24. To Be Her Refuge

I want her to choose me,
Not from obligation or need,
But with the softness of her heart,
In a moment where silence speaks.

I long for her eyes to find,
In mine, a shelter from the storm,
To see the refuge that I build,
With hands that ache to keep her warm.

I want her to choose me,
Not because I ask or plead,
But because in every quiet breath,
She feels I'm where she's meant to be.

I wish to be the one she turns to,
When the world is loud and cold,
To hold her when the lights grow dim,
To love her fiercely as we grow old.

For in her choosing, I would find,
A peace that no words could name,
A love that lives in sacred space,
Where both our souls ignite the flame.

25. Death Is Simple, Love Is Not

I do not fear the cold of death,
Its silence calls without deceit,
No lies to weave, no hearts to break,
Just endless dark, a calm retreat.

But love, oh love, it trembles deep,
With tender hands that shape my soul,
It promises, yet fails to keep,
The fractured heart it claims to hold.

Death is simple, death is still,
It knows no cruel or shifting tides,
But love is wild, a storm to feel,
That sweeps me up and then divides.

Attachments thread through fragile bones,
They root within, they pull, they bind,
Till love, once sweet, becomes a stone,
That drags me through the endless mind.

I fear not death, it cannot sting,
But love, it twists with blades unseen,
It leaves me raw, unraveling,
A fleeting dream, once pure, once clean.

26. Lost in the Dawn

I saw her there, in dream's embrace,
Her voice was soft, her gentle face.
She said, "I'll never hurt you more,"
A love I knew, but longed for more.

I held her tight, my heart at peace,
A kiss that made the world release.
The warmth, the touch, it felt so true,
As if the night was made for two.

But then the chime, the morning's call,
Awoke me from that dreamlike fall.
I reached for her, but she was gone,
A fleeting love, the dawn upon.

27. Footprints in the Sand

I stand where the sea meets the land,
On the shores of pain, where silence commands.
Waves crash like echoes of forgotten screams,
Eroding the heart with broken dreams.

The wind whispers tales of sorrow and loss,
Each gust a reminder of what love costs.
Footprints fade, like memories worn thin,
As the tide pulls me deeper within.

The sky above, a canvas of gray,
Reflects the tears I've hidden away.
Yet in this vast, endless sea of despair,
Hope is a distant, shimmering flare.

But here at the edge, where pain holds sway,
I know that even the darkest day,
Must yield to the dawn, however faint,
As the soul learns to heal, learns to paint.

So I linger a moment, on this mournful strand,
Letting the pain slip from my hand,
For even at the shores of deepest sorrow,
There lies the promise of a brighter tomorrow.

28. Pure as Light

Love, for me, is a quiet flame,
A whisper that softly calls her name.
It's not possession, nor a claim,
But a feeling pure, with no need for fame.

It's in her smile, the way it glows,
In every moment, how her essence shows.
It's not about "mine," or what could be,
But the joy she brings, effortlessly.

Love is patience, a silent prayer,
Hoping she's happy, beyond compare.
It's not in words but in the heart,
A melody playing, when we're apart

For me, love is simply this:
A gentle hope, a timeless bliss.
No bounds, no labels, just being true,
To cherish her light, the way I do.

29. The Sweetest Theft

Under the stars in the midnight hue,
I stand here trembling, thinking of you.
Each heartbeat speaks what words can't say,
You've stolen my soul in the sweetest way.

Your laughter's a song, your smile a flame,
Each moment with you, I'm never the same.
The world fades to shadows when you are near,
For in your presence, all's bright and clear.

O darling, my heart beats loud and true,
Every rhythm it hums is for only you.
Your eyes hold the magic of dreams untold,
A treasure far more than silver or gold.
I kneel before you, my words take flight,
Will you be my dawn, my star, my light?
Together, let's write a story divine,
Say yes, my love, and forever be mine.

30. The Final Piece

I walked through life, a fractured whole,
With empty spaces in my soul.
A thousand pieces, scattered wide,
Yet none could fill the void inside.

I tried to mend, to patch, to bind,
But something vital stayed behind.
A picture blurred, a story untold,
A puzzle yearning to unfold.

And then there you were, quiet, clear,
The piece I'd sought through every year.
You didn't force, you didn't fight,
You simply fit perfect, right.

With you, the chaos turned to art,
A masterpiece within my heart.
The gaps were gone, the cracks erased,
Each broken shard in you replaced.

Now, I am whole, my search complete,
With every line and edge replete.
For in your love, I found my peace,
You were always the final piece.

31. In the Shadows

I willingly choose to live unseen,
In quiet realms, where silence reigns,
Where sunlight fades, and moonlight's gleam,
Is the only guide through endless plains.

No spotlight shines upon my way,
No praise, no cheers, no grand display.
Yet in the shadows, I find my place,
A hidden path, a nameless face.

I need no fame, no crown to wear,
For what I guard is far more rare.
A truth, a cause, a sacred call,
For which I rise, for which I fall.

In whispered winds, my vow is cast,
To hold the future, heal the past.
And though the world may never know,
In shadows deep, I choose to grow.

For strength is found in places still,
Beyond the light, beyond the thrill.
I walk alone, yet never stray,
In the shadows, I choose to stay.

32. The War Within

My mind paints her in shades of grey,
A storm that clouds each passing day,
With reasons sharp, it draws the line,
Whispers, "She is not for you this time."

Yet my heart, a rebel, beats her name,
In every rhythm, it's just the same,
It sings her tune, it knows her well,
In love's sweet trap, it dares to dwell.

My mind says flee, forget, move on,
But my heart clings to her at dawn,
In every breath, in every sigh,
Her memory lives, it won't deny.

I'm torn in two, I fight, I fall,
Between the logic and the call,
Of love that lingers, pure and true,
Though my mind says she's not for you.

But can I choose, can I decide,
When heart and mind are so divided?
One loves, one fears, yet both are me,
Lost in this endless dichotomy.

33. Farewell

Nothing makes the past a sweeter place,
Than the whisper of death's tender trace.
When life's final curtain draws near,
Memories bloom, vivid and clear.

Forgotten moments rise to the fore,
Old wounds soften, hurt no more.
Laughter echoes, brighter than before,
In the face of time's closing door.

The past, once a shadow, now gleams,
Bathed in the light of near ending dreams.
Imminent death, with its quiet grace,
Turns every memory into a sacred space.

So we linger, in those days of yore,
Finding comfort in what came before.
For nothing makes the past so sweet,
As the knowledge of life's fleeting beat.

34. Scars of an Endless War

A storm brews deep within my chest,
A restless sea that won't find rest.
Waves of doubt and tides of fear,
Crash and swell, ever near.

A war between the heart and mind,
In tangled thoughts, I'm confined.
The voice of reason, calm and clear,
Battles whispers I can't ignore or steer.

One side calls for peace and light,
To lay down arms, end the fight.
But shadows rise with every breath,
Whispering tales of pain and death.

My heart beats with a warrior's might,
Yet falters in the darkest night.
It yearns for peace, a quiet shore,
But finds itself in endless war.

The mind, a soldier, sharp and cold,
Wants to conquer, to control.
It draws its blade of logic keen,
Cutting through emotions, unseen.

But the heart, it bleeds and won't relent,

In every wound, it finds lament.
For love and hope, it fights in vain,
Against the mind's unyielding chain.

The battle rages, day and night,
A constant struggle, a silent fight.
No victor crowned, no peace to find,
Just the scars of war left behind.

I'm torn between what's right and true,
And what my heart demands I do.
A battle within that none can see,
A fight that's fought eternally.

But in the depths of this inner war,
I find the strength to endure once more.
For though the battle never ends,
I stand my ground, no need to pretend.

I'll walk this path, with head held high,
Through storms that rage and darkened sky.
For in this battle, I'll find my way,
And live to fight another day.

35. Once a Dream, Now a Curse

I loved you once with all my heart,
A flame so bright, it burned apart.
Every word, every glance, every touch,
In you, I found my world, my crutch.

But love, it seems, can swiftly turn,
To ashes cold from fires that burn.
Now the thought of you brings fear,
A shadowed past that haunts me here.

You were my dream, my sweetest song,
A melody where I belonged.
But now, your name is a bitter sound,
A nightmare in which I drown.

The hands that once held me close,
Now grip my throat like tightening ropes.
Your voice, a whisper in the dark,
Cuts through my soul, leaves a mark.

I try to forget, to banish your face,
But memories linger, they won't erase.
You're the ghost in the corners of my mind,
A haunting presence I can't leave behind.

I loved you the most, with all I had,

But now, that love has turned so bad.
Afraid to remember, I bury it deep,
Hoping in time, it will finally sleep.

But even in dreams, you find your way,
Turning my nights into endless gray.
You were my light, but now you're the night,
A darkened path, no end in sight.

So here I stand, on shattered ground,
Once lost in love, now painfully found.
From loving you the most, I've come to fear,
The memory of you that lingers near.

36. Dancing Through the Pain

We all wear smiles, say we're fine,
In the light, we let our laughter shine,
But deep inside, shadows linger near,
No, my dear, we're all liars here.

We speak of joy, of carefree days,
Yet carry burdens in hidden ways.
Our hearts, they ache with silent cries,
Behind each smile, a truth denies.

We dance in the sun, play the part,
But there's a storm within each heart.
We say we're happy, full of cheer,
But no, my dear, we lie out of fear.

For to show the cracks, to be exposed,
Is to reveal the pain we've enclosed.
So we wear the mask, hold back the tears,
And lie, my dear, to silence our fears.

37. Dreams and Reality

In the quiet of the night, I dream,
Of paths we might have walked,
Beneath the stars' gentle gleam,
Where hearts could have softly talked.

Though time has wandered far away,
And days have turned to years,
My heart still holds that yesterday,
And the hope it still endears.

I see your smile in every dawn,
Your voice in every breeze,
In moments when I'm most withdrawn,
Your memory brings me ease.

The world moves on, yet here I stay,
In this space of "might have been,"
Still hoping that you'll come my way,
And we'll find what's lost again.

38. Searching for You

My eyes are constantly searching for you,
Through endless skies of deepest blue,
In every shadow, every light,
They wander, longing for your sight.

They trace the stars that softly gleam,
And chase the whispers of a dream,
Through crowded streets or quiet lanes,
In every drop of summer's rains.

They seek you in the morning's glow,
In every place the winds might blow,
In autumn leaves that dance and fall,
In winter's hush, they heed your call.

My eyes are restless, never still,
They wander wide against my will,
For in this world so vast and wide,
They only wish to find your side.

39. Empty Words, Empty Space

You promised me forever, yet here I stand alone,
In the echoes of your words, a vow now turned to stone.
You said no fight could sever the bond that we once knew,
But now the space beside me is empty, just like you.

We danced in whispered promises, held tight against the night,
And in your eyes, I trusted that we would be alright.
But somewhere in the silence, the distance grew too wide,
And all the words you whispered were swept out with the tide.

You left me with a question, a pain I can't set free,
Why did you walk away when you swore you'd stay with me?
The answers lie in shadows, where broken promises dwell,
And in the ache of knowing, I loved you all too well.

So now I stand in quiet, with only memories to keep,
Of a love that once was promised, but now has gone to sleep.
You left me with your silence, where once your words would weave,
A story of forever that you were first to leave.

40. Fallen Petals

In the garden where trust once bloomed,
Whispers of betrayal loom.
Petals fall from flowers bright,
Dimming love's once radiant light.

Eyes that sparkled, now they lie,
Hiding truths, weaving sighs.
Promises, like fragile threads,
Unraveled into silent dreads.

The touch that once a comfort gave,
Now a chill, a breaking wave.
Words of love, now tainted, cold,
A story altered, lies unfold

In shadows deep, a heart now breaks,
Echoes of the trust it stakes.
Tears, like rivers, carve their way,
Through the soul, now led astray.

Once a refuge, now a storm,
Trust and love in disarray, torn.
Betrayal from the dearest one,
A dark eclipse of love's bright sun.

41. Men do cry

Beneath the armor, hearts are bare,
With fragile dreams and silent cries,
The myths of men in Tearless Nights,
Are shattered when the heart complies.

In quiet rooms, in darkest hours,
The weight of worlds can bring them low,
A father's fear, a lover's loss,
Their tears like rivers start to flow.

They weep for friendships lost to time,
For failures haunting restless sleep,
For children grown and dreams unmade,
For promises they couldn't keep.

Their eyes may glisten at a song,
Or at the sight of newborn grace,
A tender moment, raw and real,
Brings tears that trace an honest face.

For every drop, a story told,
Of love, of grief, of joy, of strife,
These tears are proof of beating hearts,
Of souls that live a human life.

So, let the world embrace this truth,
And break the chains of stoic lies,

For men do cry, and in their tears,
We find the light in human skies.

• 47 •

42. A melody in endless play

In the quiet of the evening's hush,
Where shadows dance and daylight fades,
Feelings bloom in a tender rush,
Weaving through the twilight's shades.

Joy, a burst of sunlight bright,
Warms the heart with a golden glow,
Spreading wings in a boundless flight,
In realms where dreams and hopes flow.

Sorrow, a whisper soft and low,
Paints the world in hues of gray,
A river of tears in a gentle flow,
Washing pain and fears away.

Love, a fire that softly burns,
Ignites the soul with passionate flame,
In every heart's deep, secret turns,
Echoes a cherished, whispered name.

Anger, a storm in a fierce embrace,
Roars with thunder, fierce and wild,
Yet fades away, leaving no trace,
A fleeting tempest briefly riled

Peace, a lullaby's gentle call,
Cradles the weary in its arms,

A balm that soothes and heals all,
With its quiet, tender charms.

Feelings, a symphony of life's design,
Compose the song of every day,
In each heart's intricate line,
A melody in endless play.

43. Restless Mind

In labyrinths of thoughts, I, roam,
A restless mind, my only home.
With every question, doubts entwine,
A web of worries that, are mine.

I wander paths both old and new,
In search of truths that won't break through.
Each choice was dissected, parsed, and weighed,
In endless loops, my thoughts are swayed.

What if, what then, what might have been?
My restless spirit is trapped within.
A cascade of "what should I do?"
A storm of "if" that clouds my view.

Yet in these depths, a keen insight,
A spark that flickers in the night.
When I think and think again;
I find the beauty in the pain.

My heart may ache, my mind may spin,
But treasures lie concealed within.
For through the haze, I often see,
A deeper truth, a clarity.

So, in this maze where I may ponder,

I'll seek new worlds and sometimes wander.
And though my mind may never cease,
I'll find a path to my own peace.

• 51 •

44. Beyond the Hurt

You wounded me with words unkind,
Left scars and echoes in my mind.
But still, my love for you remains,
A tether through our joys and pains.

Forgiveness blooms, a fragile rose,
In the garden where our story grows.
Though tears have fallen like the rain,
Love whispers softly through the pain.

I choose to see beyond the night,
To where our hearts can find the light.
In letting go, I find the peace,
A silent prayer for sweet release.

For love, it bears the weight of all,
It lifts us when we start to fall.
And though you hurt me, I forgive,
For in this grace, our hearts can live.

45. The Mask I Wear

I'm not okay, but I wear a smile,
Hiding pain beneath each mile,
A facade so carefully built,
Covering layers of sorrow and guilt.

Eyes that shimmer with unshed tears,
Masked by laughter that no one hears,
In the silence, my heart does break,
A whispering ache, a persistent quake.

The weight of worries, a silent load,
Beneath the surface, emotions explode,
Yet, to the world, I seem just fine,
A well-practiced lie in every line.

Inside, the storm rages on,
A battle fought from dusk till dawn,
But still, I rise, greet each day,
For hope, perhaps, will find its way.

I'm not okay, but I carry on,
Waiting for the night to meet the dawn,
In the darkness, I find my fight,
Dreams of light in the endless night.

46. A Song Left Unfinished

In the quiet corners of our shared life,
Where whispers danced and shadows thrived,
She gazed at me with puzzled eyes,
A love so deep, but in disguise.

I wove my heart with threads of care,
In gestures small and moments rare,
But in her eyes, a yearning gleamed,
For love in ways I never dreamed.

She sought the words I left unspoken,
In tender vows, her heart was broken,
While I believed in acts, not phrases,
Her longing burned in silent phases.

Her love was wrapped in crystal glass,
Fragile, needing touch to pass,
Yet I, with hands of iron, strong,
Held her close but held it wrong.

We stood on the shores of different seas,
Her tides were soft, mine rough with pleas,
I failed to see her silent plea,
She failed to feel the heart in me.

Our Love, a song in different keys,
A symphony that couldn't please,

Two souls that danced but never met,
A love that lingers with regret.

Now echoes of what could have been,
Float in the air, a mournful hymn,
She failed to grasp my silent art,
I failed to love her tender heart.

47. A Quiet Storm

In every breath, a subtle sting,
A whisper of despair it brings.
The light feels distant, hard to find,
As darkness settles in my mind.

Each day, a battle is fought within,
A war where neither side can win.
The smile I wear, a thin disguise,
To hide the tears behind my eyes.

It's killing me slowly, piece by piece,
A quiet storm that will not cease.
Yet in this struggle, I'll persist,
For somewhere, hope and light exist.

48. Silent Scream

There's a pain that words can't touch,
Silent, deep, it hurts too much.
A shadow dark, a whispered cry,
Hidden tear in the mind's eye.

It sits behind a smiling face,
A heart encased in fragile grace.
A burden carried, never shown,
A sorrow felt when all alone.

It's the ache that time can't heal,
A wound unseen, but deeply real.
A silent scream within the chest,
A yearning ache, a soul's unrest.

Invisible, it roams the night,
An endless fight, an unseen plight.
No words to shape, no voice to tell,
This quiet, haunting, private hell.

49. The brain and heart

In chambers deep, where thoughts reside,
The brain, a fortress, logic's guide,
With reason sharp and clear as day,
It maps the path, it charts the way.

But in the depths, where passions start,
There beats a drum, the fervent heart,
With fervor wild and whispers sweet,
It dances to an untamed beat.

The brain declares, "Stay on the ground,
For paths of risk are seldom sound,
With measured steps and cautious tread,
We'll find our way, avoid the dread."

The heart replies, "But life's a song,
A melody where we belong,
In leaps of faith, in loves we chase,
We find the joy, we find our place."

The brain insists, "But pain is real,
It's wiser not to feel and heal,
Emotions cloud, they lead astray,
They turn the night into the day.

The heart responds, "Yet love's the light,
That turns the dark to sheer delight,

Without its flame, what is the worth,
Of living days upon this earth?"

In a constant clash, they fight, they blend,
Two voices that will never bend,
Yet in their dance, we find our soul,
A harmony that makes us whole.

For reason's mind and passion's art,
Both play a part, both own the chart,
Together bound, though worlds apart,
The brain and heart, the brain and heart.

50. The Heart That Gives

In shadows cast by twilight's gleam,
Love stands beyond the dreamer's dream.
Its essence pure, its heart so wise,
Revealed through selfless sacrifice.

It's not in gifts or grand displays,
Nor spoken in a thousand ways.
It's in the quiet, steadfast hand,
That offers all, yet makes no stand.

Love's true form, a tender grace,
Reflected in a humble face.
A silent tear, a gentle sigh,
The strength to let the moment fly.

To give, expecting no return,
In passion's fire, to let it burn.
A whispered prayer, a stifled cry,
For other's joy, to self-deny.

It's found in nights of sleepless care,
In burdens that two hearts can bear.
In every choice that sets one free,
In every whisper, "Come to me."

For love is not an easy road,

It's bearing up another's load.
In giving all, our hearts align,
In sacrifice, love's light will shine.

So let us walk this sacred path,
Embrace its trials, endure its wrath.
For in the giving, we receive,
And in our sacrifice, believe.

51. A New Road Ahead

Echoes of laughter, whispers of plans,
Now dissolve in shifting sands.
The vision bright, now shadow's friend,
A story's arc that didn't bend.

The castle was built in clouds so high,
Now crumbles as the days go by.
The plans I made with fervent zeal,
Now fade, as dreams are no longer real.

It's hard to let the vision go,
The life I thought I'd come to know.
But in the loss, I find a space,
To weave new dreams with quiet grace.

The world is vast, with turns unseen,
With other hopes and fields of green.
And though this road diverges far,
I'll follow where new dreams are.

For every ending births a start,
A chance to heal a broken heart.
To find the beauty in the pain,
To dance once more in life's refrain.

So here I stand, with open eyes,

Beneath the ever-changing skies.
The life I dreamed of may not be mine,
But other stars will surely shine.

In every tear, a lesson learned,
In every loss, a corner turned
And though the dream I held has flown,
In its place, a strength I've grown.

For life, though different than it seemed,
Can hold new joys, yet undreamed.
And in this truth, I'll find my way,
To live, to love, another day.

52. Vengeance

Betrayal's sting, a wound so deep,
A trust now shattered, vows to weep,
In shadows dark, where anguish lies,
A seed of vengeance slowly thrives.

You turned away, a knife in hand,
And left me in a broken land,
A friend once close, now enemy,
A tale of hurt, of treachery.

In silence, I will bide my time,
Injustice met with measured rhyme,
The fire within, burns so bright,
A beacon in the darkest night.

I'll rise from ashes, cold and gray,
And plot the course to make you pay,
For every lie, for every tear,
I'll bring to light your darkest fear.

No mercy found in my cold gaze,
A reckoning in countless ways,
The hurt you dealt will circle back,
A storm unleashed a fierce attack.

But in the heart where vengeance brews,
A deeper truth will start to fuse,

That seeking pain for pain received,
Leaves both the scarred and the bereaved.

So though I crave to see you fall,
I grasp the weight, the cost of all,
Perhaps in time, this rage will wane,
And from my heart, release the pain.

For in forgiveness, strength is found,
A peace that heals, a love unbound,
Yet should you cross my path once more,
Remember well the score we bore.

53. A Promise to Myself

To the mirror where my soul reflects,
I offer words, a heart's deep dialects,
For every shadow cast on my name,
I pen this verse, releasing all my shame.

I'm sorry for the times I turned away,
From dreams that begged to see the light of day,
For moments when I silenced my voice,
Forgetting that I always had a choice.

Forgive me for the harsh words I've spoken,
To the spirit within that now feels broken,
For doubting my worth in the darkest night,
And hiding my truth from the world's sight.

I'm sorry for the battles fought alone,
For wearing masks and hearts of stone,
For all the tears I did not let fall,
And the burdens are borne without a call.

But now I stand with open arms, contrite,
Embracing flaws and strengths alike,
A promise to be kinder, true,
To honor the journey that is uniquely you.

I'll nurture dreams with tender care,
And give my soul the space to dare,

To live, to love, to grow, to be,
An endless voyage to set me free.

So here's to the past and lessons learned,
To self-compassion, hard-earned,
In this apology, I find release,
A pledge to walk in self-love and peace.

54. One more time

I want to try once more, to chase the dawn,
To find the light where shadows have withdrawn.
With heart unyielding and spirit bold,
I'll forge ahead, and let new stories unfold.

I want to try once more, with lessons learned,
From every fall, and every bridge I've burned.
With eyes set forward, and past behind,
I'll seek the dreams that once seemed hard to find.

I want to try once more, to touch the sky,
To rise from where I've fallen, reach up high.
With every setback, the stronger I'll become,
For in each trial, my spirit is the drum.

I want to try once more, and feel the fire,
That burns within, a flame of pure desire.
With every step, no matter how unsure,
I'll pave a path where hope and faith endure.

I want to try once more, and seize the day,
To write my story in a brighter way.
With courage bold, and dreams that never die,
I'll spread my wings again, and learn to fly.

55. The mortal gate

Death is coming, softly near,
An echo of the end we fear.
A gentle touch, a quiet sigh,
The final gaze, the last goodbye.

Death is coming, sure and slow,
A river's flow we all must know.
But in its wake, peace is profound
in silent sleep, we are unbound.

Death is coming, silent tread,
A whisper in the winds we dread.
Shadows lengthen, day grows dim,
Life's bright candle flickers thin.
No door can bar, no lock can bind,
It slips unseen through heart and mind.
A cold embrace, a final kiss,
In death's dark arms, eternal bliss.
Yet fear not this inevitable night,
For in its depths, a hidden light.
Beyond the veil, new worlds await,
A journey past the mortal gate.

Epilogue

And so, Grief's Melody comes to a close,
Fifty-five verses, each a heartbeat,
Each thread is woven from sorrow and light,
Echoes of a soul learning to breathe again.
Through loss and longing, through quiet tears,
Every word was a step toward healing.
Pain etched into ink, shaped into rhythm,
Transformed beneath the weight of truth.
Grief may have been the muse,
But love and hope became the melody.
For in each trembling line,
A quiet strength was born.
These poems were not just written,
They lived, and they survived.
And though this chapter fades into silence,
The music of healing will always remain.
The story does not end here,
For where grief softens,
New verses will rise.
New stanzas will hum beneath the stars.
And when the heart feels heavy again,
When shadows creep upon the edge of light,
I will return to the quiet of the page,
And let the melody play once more.

A Poet's Thank You

Dear Readers,

I am truly grateful for each and every one of you who took the time to read Grief's Melody. This collection of poems is a reflection of life's highs and lows, the quiet moments of sorrow, the flickers of hope, and the strength found in between. Your support, love, and connection to these words mean more than I can express.

Poetry has a way of touching the soul, and knowing that my words have resonated with you fills me with immense gratitude. Every message, every review, and every shared thought has inspired me to keep writing. This is just the beginning, I promise to return with more verses, more emotions, and more stories in the books to come.

From the bottom of my heart, thank you for being part of this journey. Here's to many more poems and shared moments together!

With love and gratitude,

-Karthik koppi.

Help Me Perfect Every Word

Dear Readers,

Thank you for reading Grief's Melody. I poured my heart into this collection of poems, and your support means everything to me.

While every effort has been made to present this book as perfectly as possible, I understand that mistakes can sometimes slip through. If you happen to spot any errors or inconsistencies, I would be truly grateful if you could let me know. Your feedback will help me improve and ensure that future editions reflect the best possible version of this work.

Please feel free to reach out to me at karthikkoppi9@gmail.com with any corrections or suggestions. Your time and effort in helping me refine this book are deeply appreciated.

Thank you once again for being part of this journey. Your support and understanding mean the world to me.

With gratitude,
Karthik Koppi.